# TERRY LABONTE

Greg Roza

**PowerKiDS** press™

New York

Published in 2007 by The Rosen Publishing Group, Inc.
29 East 21st Street, New York, NY 10010

Book Design: Michael J. Flynn

Photo Credits: Cover (Labonte) © Craig Jones/Getty Images; cover (background) © Robert Laberge/Allsport; pp. 5, 7, 9, 13 © Rusty Jarrett/Getty Images; p. 11 © Jamie Squire/ Getty Images; pp. 15, 17 © David Taylor/Getty Images; p. 19 © Donald Miralle/Allsport; p. 21 © Craig Jones/Allsport.

Library of Congress Cataloging-in-Publication Data

Roza, Greg.
    Terry Labonte / Greg Roza.
        p. cm. — (NASCAR champions)
    Includes bibliographical references and index.
    ISBN-13: 978-1-4042-3501-9
    ISBN-10: 1-4042-3501-9 (library binding)
    1. Labonte, Terry, 1956-    . 2. Stock car drivers—United States
—Biography—Juvenile literature.    I. Title. II. Series.
    GV1032.L325R68 2007
    796.72092—dc22
    (B)
                                                                    2006014306

Manufactured in the United States of America

"NASCAR" is a registered trademark of the National Association for Stock Car Auto Racing, Inc.

# Contents

Terry Labonte is a race car driver. He races stock cars.

Terry was born in Corpus Christi, Texas. Now he lives in Thomasville, North Carolina.

Terry started racing small race cars when he was just 7. He won his first race when he was 9.

9

Terry started driving in NASCAR races in 1978. He won his first NASCAR race in 1980.

11

Terry won his first NASCAR championship in 1984. He was 27 years old.

13

Terry won a NASCAR championship again in 1996.

1996
NASCAR
Winston Cup
Champion

NASCAR WINSTON CUP SERIES SINCE 1971

PAY TO THE ORDER OF _Terry Labonte_          $1,500,000.00

_One Million Five Hundred Thousand_ DOLLARS

FOR _1996 Championship_ FROM

15

Terry's brother Bobby also drives cars in NASCAR races.

17

Terry and Bobby are the only brothers to have both won a NASCAR championship. Bobby won in 2000.

2000
NASCAR WINSTON CUP CHAMPION
BOBBY LABONTE

19

Terry is on the list of NASCAR's 50 Greatest Drivers.

# Glossary

**championship** (CHAM-pea-uhn-ship)
A contest held to see who is the best
in a sport.

**Corpus Christi** (KOHR-puhs KRIS-tee)
A city in eastern Texas.

**stock car** (STAHK KAHR)  A race car that
looks like the cars people drive on
the road.

# Books and Web Sites

## Books

Buckley, James. *NASCAR*. New York: DK Children, 2005.

Hubbard-Brown, Janet. *The Labonte Brothers*. New York: Chelsea House, 2005.

## Web Sites

Due to the changing nature of Internet links, PowerKids Press has developed an online list of Web sites related to the subject of this book. This site is updated regularly. Please use this link to access the list:
http://www.powerkidslinks.com/NASCAR/labonte/

# Index